FRENCH
à la Cartoon

Edited by
Albert H. Small, Ph.D.

HARRAP

Dedicated to
Sylvia
My First and Best Audience

And with Special Thanks to
Monique Cossard and Andrée Werlin
Who Provided Help When It Was Needed
from Both Sides of the Ocean

ISBN 0 245-54898-X

Published in this edition 1989 by Harrap Books Ltd.,
43-45 Annandale Street, Edinburgh EH7 4AZ
by arrangement with NTC Publishing Group.

©1989 NTC Publishing Group.

Reprinted 1992

Contents

A—Careful!—Word in Advance	iv
A Technical Comment—or Two	vii
The Pronouns	viii
Three Important Verbs	x
The Little Words	xi
Introducing . . . the Artists!	xiii
Cartoons	1
French-English Glossary	103
English-French Glossary	109
English-French Subject Index	115

A—Careful!—Word in Advance

A British tourist, visiting a seaside hotel in France with her family, approached the proprietor in the evening with a request. After hastily consulting her French-English dictionary, she announced: "I have only two ears. That's enough for myself and my husband, but we need an extra ear for our daughter."

She correctly suspected that she had made a mistake in her French when the laughing proprietor asked her to repeat what she had said for the benefit of his friends. In glancing at the dictionary she had confused the French word for *pillow (oreiller)* with the word for *ear (oreille).*

English-speakers learning French often fall into such pitfalls. After all, even much of the grammar seems almost the same between the two languages: *Nous avons dit cela* seems to translate directly into "We have said that." So the unsuspecting student of French isn't prepared for such subtleties as "sensitive" translating into French as *sensible* or "suntanned" becoming "bronzed"—*bronzé.* Or the insulation around an electric wire being referred to in French as *isolation.*

Things become even more confusing when French expressions used in English mean something different in France. A woman trying to buy a *brassière*, for example, would find herself being offered a baby's vest!

At the same time, the French have taken some English words or expressions and put them to strange use. A smoking jacket became *un smoking*—without the word *jacket* added—and actually refers to a tuxedo. A cocktail party is simply *un cocktail.*

Sometimes a word travels back and forth between English and French. The English "riding coat" slipped into French with a kind of French phonetic spelling as *redingote.* When women's stylists applied the term to a type of long jacket, the word returned to English with this new meaning—and with the French spelling!

Speaking of spelling, English and French sometimes slip out of synchronization on the same word. The English word *connoisseur*—someone with knowledge and discernment in a particular field—comes from an old French spelling. The same word in French today follows modern French spelling:

connaisseur. On the other hand, *ambiance,* a word taken into English directly from French, and referring to the atmosphere of a place such as a hotel or restaurant, can be spelled in English either in the original form or with the more typical English spelling "ambience."

Pronunciation can completely disguise an English word or name when used in French: Ivanhoe, pronounced "EYE-van-hoe" in English, becomes "ee-van-oe-eh" in French. The American detergent Tide, sold in France under the same name, is pronounced "Teed" over there.

Some French habits of speech are not used in English. An American, stating an opinion, is not likely to say "Me, I like the movies." But in France the equivalent—*Moi, j'aime le cinema*—would be typical conversational style. And, by the way, after you knock on the door and a member of the family asks from inside "Who is it?" you will probably say "It's me," although English grammar ordains "It is I" as the correct response. In French, relax—*C'est moi* is OK. And OK is OK in French.

Don't forget that French people "have" what English-speaking people "are"—in some respects. An English child proudly says "I am six years old," but the French child would say "I have six years"—*J'ai six ans.* Also, in French be sure to say "I have heat" *(J'ai chaud)* if you are warm or "I have hunger" *(J'ai faim).* And watch the pronunciation. The man who said *j'ai grand faim* but incorrectly pronounced the "m" in *faim* was actually saying *J'ai grande femme*—in effect "I have a big wife"!

As you will see in this book, humour can translate wonderfully well from French to English. But puns are another matter. Puns are, after all, a play on words. In English, when a Christmas tree is delivered to the wrong ship you can say the delivery person was "treeing up the wrong barque"—but you can't translate that pun into French. Once in a while, though, a play on words can be translated. When an unlucky poker player in the Old West was the victim of a bullet from the dealer's gun he could say *Quand j'ai dit "tirez" j'ai voulu dire les cartes.* In English or in French this means "When I said 'draw,' I meant the cards."

The cartoons in this book were chosen because the humor can be translated into English from French. For example, you

can say in English *or* in French that a not-too-bright fellow
has "nothing between the ears," and one of our French
cartoonists illustrates the point.

But note well: the literal translation and the *Everyday
English* caption at the bottom of the page can be far apart. In
effect, what we have sometimes done is to recaption the
cartoon as an English editor might in adapting a French
cartoon for an English newspaper or magazine. This not only
improves the joke, but often sharply illustrates the difference
between French and English conversational idioms. And
that's one of the purposes of the book: to help take you away
from the routine rules of syntax and vocabulary, and bring
you out to the world of people speaking French in ordinary
situations.

Why choose humour as a learning aid? Obviously because
humour is an enjoyable way for getting anything done. But
more than that, the key to learning is *memory*—and for
almost everybody there is nothing more memorable than a
really good joke.

So please don't blame us if you remember the French
expression for a ship's engine room because the speaking
tube in the pilot house is spouting oil in the first mate's face,
or if the expression for "fine weather" stays in your mind
because the rain has put out the fire under the fellow who
was to be burned at the stake. You may even learn how to say
"hands up" in French because the woman is scaring the
burglars by yelling at them through the drain pipe!

Good reading—and good laughing!

A Technical Comment—or Two

Learning a language can be fun, especially when it helps you understand the punch line of a joke or the conversation at a get-together. But let's face it—learning a language can also get complicated. In this book we're going to try to keep as much of the fun as we can, and burden you with a minimum of complications.

Basically, the vocabulary provided in this book is an aid to understanding the cartoons. We won't give you *all* the possible translations of a French word—just the ones that relate to the material at hand.

We won't bother translating the words you can figure out for yourself—even in cases where the spelling differs somewhat from the spelling in English. But please be alert for the different ways in which such words can be used in French. *Banal* in English, for example, is a relatively erudite word for something that is commonplace or spiritless; although the meaning in French can be similar, the word is used in ordinary conversation in the way we might refer to something as "trite" or "unoriginal."

Incidentally, we've used some fairly obvious abbreviations: *n.* for noun, *adj.* for adjective, *adv.* for adverb, *v.* for verb, *inf.* for infinitive, *conj.* for conjunction, *m.* for masculine, *f.* for feminine. To help you recognize a verb in other usages, we add the infinitive form (when the infinitive isn't used in the cartoon caption) along with the verb form that is used.

To avoid cluttering up the vocabulary list under each cartoon, we've written three sections to handle the most common words. **Pronouns** are an especially important part of everyday speech, so you will want to be familiar with the common ones. Then, the **Three Important Verbs**—French for "to be," "to have," and "to go"—are important for themselves and as helper verbs, just as in English. You will want to recognize all their forms on sight. Finally, **The Little Words** are the ones that link together ordinary speech—words like *the, but, here, everybody,* and so forth. Rather than listing these words every time they appear on a cartoon caption, we've brought them together in this list to encourage you to make sure they are a basic part of your French vocabulary.

The Pronouns

This is not an exhaustive list of pronouns in French. Rather, it is an illustration of how common pronouns you will encounter in the cartoon captions can be used in conversation.

Subject Pronouns

Je parle.	**I** talk.
Tu parles.	**You** (sing., familiar) talk.
Il parle.	**He** talks.
Elle parle.	**She** talks.
Nous parlons.	**We** talk.
Vous parlez.	**You** (pl., formal) talk.
Ils parlent.	**They** (m.) talk.
Elles parlent.	**They** (f.) talk.

Direct Object Pronouns

Elle **me** voit.	She sees **me.**
Elle **te** voit.	She sees **you** (sing., familiar).
Je **le** vois.	I see **him.**
Je **la** vois.	I see **her.**
Elle **nous** voit.	She sees **us.**
Elle **vous** voit.	She sees **you** (pl., formal).
Je **les** vois.	I see **them.**

Indirect Object Pronouns

Il **me** donne le crayon.	He gives **me** the pencil.
Il **te** donne le crayon.	He gives **you** (sing., familiar) the pencil.
Je **lui** donne le crayon.	I give **him, her** the pencil.
Il **nous** donne le crayon.	He gives **us** the pencil.
Je **vous** donne le crayon.	I give **you** (pl., formal) the pencil.
Je **leur** donne le crayon.	I give **them** the pencil.

Double Object Pronouns

Elle **me le** donne.	She gives **it to me**.
Elle **te le** donne.	She gives **it to you** (sing., familiar).
Je **le lui** donne.	I give **it to him, her**.
Elle **nous le** donne.	She gives **it to us**.
Je **vous le** donne.	I give **it to you** (pl., formal).
Je **le leur** donne.	I give **it to them**.

Two Relative Pronouns

C'est mon frère **qui** téléphone.	It's my brother **who** is calling.
C'est le musée **que** je veux voir.	It's the museum **that** I want to see.

Three Important Verbs

This is a list of three tenses commonly used in conversation. You will see them often in the cartoon captions.

être (to be)	avoir (to have)	aller (to go)
Present		
je suis	j'ai	je vais
tu es	tu as	tu vas
il, elle est	il, elle a	il, elle va
nous sommes	nous avons	nous allons
vous êtes	vous avez	vous allez
ils, elles sont	ils, elles ont	ils, elles vont
Past Perfect		
j'ai été	j'ai eu	je suis allé(e)
tu as été	tu as eu	tu es allé(e)
il, elle a été	il, elle a eu	il, elle est allé(e)
nous avons été	nous avons eu	nous sommes allé(e)s
vous avez été	vous avez eu	vous etes allé(e)s
ils, elles ont été	ils, elles ont eu	ils, elles sont allé(e)s
Future		
je serai	j'aurai	j'irai
tu seras	tu auras	tu iras
il, elle sera	il, elle aura	il, elle ira
nous serons	nous aurons	nous irons
vous serez	vous aurez	vous irez
ils, elles seront	ils, elles auront	ils, elles iront

The Little Words

A refresher on some of the common words that hold the conversation together.

à	to
après	after
avant	before
avec	with
bien	well
bientôt	soon
chaque	each
combien	how many, how much
dans	in
de, du, des	of, of the
dessous	under
dessus	above
en	in; some (as in *nous en avons,* we have some)
encore	again
enfin	at last
ensemble	together
entre	between
ici	here
là	there
le, la, les	the
mais	but
ne ... jamais	never
ne ... plus	no more

ne ... que	only
ne ... rien	nothing
on	one (as in *on ne sait jamais*, one never knows)
ou	or
où	where
parce que	because
peu	little
peut-être	perhaps
pour	for
pourtant	however
quand	when
sans	without
si	if
sous	under
souvent	often
sur	on
surtout	above all
toujours	always, still
tout le monde	everybody
très	very
trop	too, too much, too many
un, une	a, one
y	there (as in *nous y étions*, we were there)

Introducing . . . the Artists!

Robert Huet (Alexandre) says of himself: "After studying fine arts (without enthusiasm) then advertising (without conviction), I became a topographer (without great success)."

With tongue in cheek, he says that he launched his career as a cartoonist to fight a permanent and ever-increasing pessimism, and that he draws his cartoons in those rare moments of euphoria brought on by engaging in sports.

Whatever the inspiration, the results are well worth it!

André Gondot tried working as a carpenter, printer, lumberjack, and street peddler, with indifferent success in all. He served his obligatory time in the military, and detested it.

At age 23 he drew his first cartoons and saw them published within two months. Since then, thousands have appeared in the French and foreign press.

His characters are not heroes, but ordinary beings, pathetic and ridiculous in their struggle to be "tall, strong, and handsome, and to be loved." His drawings mock such people, but with humour and tenderness. "Understanding," he says, "rises out of desperation." A man reading his morning paper is more concerned about dripping coffee on his shirt than about the East-West conference headlined on page one.

Therefore Gondot does not portray the events that shape history, but rather the daily existence of his fellow citizens.

For over 40 years **André Harvec** has delighted audiences in France and other countries with an artistic output that includes posters, cartoons, comic strips, and animated features. Born in Saint-Nicolas de Redon near the Atlantic coast, he started as a lithographic artist, but soon branched out into many other fields.

Although his wonderful humour seems to be drawn from shrewd observation of the human condition, Harvec attributes his ideas instead to a particularly active imagination. Talkative in person, Harvec prefers that the characters in his cartoons say very little, and his favorites are the cartoons where the humour comes across entirely without words.

Despite his great creative output, Harvec still finds time

for his many hobbies: skiing, cycling in the mountains, colour photography, and do-it-yourself projects.

José Tricot points out that a cartoonist is a truly creative person. For his inventive genius to express itself properly, his smallest wants must be catered to, just as those of a great opera singer. He must have no money worries. He needs excellent meals, served at the moment he wants them. He must drink in moderation, but only the best wines. Everyone around him must make it a point of honour to create an atmosphere of complete serenity. Above all, to relax, he must have money, silence, and his slippers.

At least that's what he's been killing himself for all these years trying to tell his editors, his tax collector, his wife and children—and his dog.

Jacques LAVERGNE says he seeks to look at the comic side of life, to laugh rather than to cry. His approach to living ("I won't depart from this world alive") is shared by his wife and son, and, over the past forty years—through thousands of his cartoons—by the readers of many of the major periodicals in France. His cartoons have also appeared in Switzerland, Germany, Belgium, Italy, Spain, and even Japan.

Now he comes to the United States.

Not too many leading cartoonists can also lay claim to expertise in aikido, the aristocratic Japanese martial art. But this is one of the accomplishments of **Michel PIÉDOUE.**

Even in his drawings, Piédoue feels that his philosophy of aikido—tinged perhaps with a bit of surrealism—is reflected in the action themes, as opposed to themes of safety and stability.

Born in Sainte Marie aux Anglais (Normandy), Piédoue is married and has two grown children, a son and a daughter. He did not expect to become a cartoonist, although he remembers sketching as a hobby even when he was quite young and tried his hand at painting when in his twenties.

His many talents include those of novelist, essayist, and translator, and his writings, cartoons, and comic strips have appeared in many of France's most prestigious publications.

PIERRE Cochet was born in eastern France (Franche-Comté) but considers himself half Parisian. He began drawing when very young but thought he would become a painter.

He and his wife often visit eastern France, where he likes to paint (as an amateur), garden, and fish. One unusual attribute: he draws with his left hand—but writes with his right!

His hobbies are the graphic arts in general and Oriental carpets.

Piédoue

—Allons mon petit Charles, dis toi-même a monsieur l'instituteur combien tu es content de venir à l'école!

Key Words

dis (*v.*, dire *inf.*)	tell
toi-meme (*pronoun*)	yourself
instituteur (*n.*, *m.*)	teacher
venir (*v.*, *inf.*)	come
école (*n.*, *f.*)	school

Everyday English

"Come on Charles, my boy, tell the teacher how happy you are to come to school!"

Harvec

—Tu m'avais pourtant promis de ne plus jouer.

Key Words

jouer (*v., inf.*)   play

Everyday English

"But you promised me not to play anymore . . ."

Lavergne

—Paraît qu'il y a une fuite de mazout dans la salle des machines, Cap'taine.

Key Words

paraît (*v.*, paraître *inf.*)	seems
fuite (*n., f.*)	leak
mazout (*n., m.*)	oil
salle des machines (*n., f.*)	engine room

Everyday English

"Seems there's an oil leak in the engine room, Captain!"

Piédoue

—Laissez-les jouer ensemble, vous verrez qu'ils deviendront vite inséparables.

Key Words

laissez (*v.*, laisser *inf.*)	let
jouer (*v.*, *inf.*)	play
verrez (*v.*, voir *inf.*)	will see
deviendront (*v.*, devenir *inf.*)	will become
vite (*adv.*)	quickly

Everyday English

"Let them play together, you'll see they will soon become inseparable!"

Gondot

—Vous voulez un acquittement après ce que vous avez fait! Ma parole, vous êtes innocent!

Key Words

voulez (*v.*, vouloir *inf.*)	want
fait (*v.*, faire *inf.*)	done
parole (*n.*, *f.*)	word

Everyday English

"You want to be acquitted after what you did! My, you *are* innocent!"

José

—Et il a des yeux de la couleur du cuir de sa Rolls . . .

Key Words

yeux (*n., m.*)   eyes
cuir (*n., m.*)   leather

Everyday English

"And he has eyes the color of the leather upholstery in his Rolls-Royce . . ."

José

—Ne craignez rien, il n'a jamais mordu un facteur . . .

Key Words

craignez (*v.*, craindre *inf.*)   be afraid of
mordu (*v.*, mordre *inf.*)   bitten
facteur (*n.*, *m.*)   postman

Everyday English

"Don't worry, he's never bitten a postman."

Pierre

—Huit jours de suspension de permis!

Key Words

huit	eight
jours (*n.*, *m.*)	days
permis (*n.*, *m.*)	license
pêche (*n.*, *f.*)	fishing

Everyday English

"Eight days suspension of your fishing license!"

Alexandre

—C'est bien trop lourd, fais donc plusieurs voyages! . . .

Key Words

lourd (*adj.*)	heavy
fais (*v.*, faire *inf.*)	make
donc (*conj.*)	therefore
plusieurs (*adj.*)	many, several
voyages (*n.*, *m.*)	trips

Everyday English

"That's much too heavy, make extra trips instead."

Harvec

—Tout d'abord, tu vas apprendre à nager...

Key Words

tout d'abord	first of all
apprendre (*v., inf.*)	learn
nager (*v., inf.*)	swim

Everyday English

"First of all, you'll have to learn to swim..."

José

—. . . Je bavarde, je bavarde, je bavarde, et on ne voit plus Saint-Tropez!

Key Words

bavarde (*v.*, bavarder *inf.*)   talk, gossip
voit (*v.*, voir *inf.*)   see

Everyday English

"I've been talking, talking, talking, and we're already out of sight of St. Tropez."

Alexandre

—J'ai bien failli rater le départ!

Key Words

départ (*n., m.*)	departure
failli (*v.*, faillir *inf.*)	came near
rater (*v., inf.*)	miss
mer (*n., f.*)	sea

Everyday English

"I almost missed the boat!"

José

—Notre groupe financier traverse de très graves difficultés.
Désormais, avec votre café, il vous sera remis un seul sucre.

Key Words

traverse (*v.*, traverser *inf.*)	undergo
désormais (*adv.*)	from now on
café (*n.*, *m.*)	coffee
remis (*v.*, remettre *inf.*)	deliver, give
seul (*adj.*)	single, only one
sucre (*n.*, *m.*)	sugar

Everyday English

"Our corporation is having serious financial problems. From
now on, you will receive only one sugar for your coffee."

Lavergne

—Bon, maintenant, à mon tour de vous poser une question. Où se trouve votre compteur à gaz? J'étais juste venu pour le relever.

Key Words

tour (*n., m.*)	turn
se trouve (*v.*, se trouver, *inf.*)	is located
compteur à gaz (*n., m.*)	gas meter
venu (*v.*, venir *inf.*)	came
relever (*v., inf.*)	take a reading

Everyday English

"Good, now it's my turn to ask a question. Where's the gas meter? I just came to read it."

José

—Alfred, la grosse poignée noire en plastique, elle débloquait la boîte à gants ou le frein à main?

Key Words

grosse (*adj.*)	big
poignée (*n., f.*)	handle
noire (*adj.*)	black
débloquait (*v.*, débloquer *inf.*)	release
boîte à gants (*n., f.*)	glove compartment
frein (*n., m.*)	brake
main (*n., f.*)	hand

Everyday English

"Alfred—the big black plastic handle—was that for the glove compartment or the hand brake?"

Piédoue

—Le Bon Dieu vous le rendra.

Key Words

agence (*n., f.*)   agency
prêts (*n., m.*)   loans
rendra (*v.,* rendre *inf.*)   will repay

Everyday English

(Sign says: Loan office.)
"The Good Lord will repay you!"

Harvec

—Le propriétaire la vend parce qu'on lui a retiré son permis de conduire pour excès de vitesse!

Key Words

propriétaire (*n., m.*)	owner
vend (*v.,* vendre *inf.*)	sell
retiré (*v.,* retirer *inf.*)	withdraw
permis de conduire (*n., m.*)	driver's license
excès (*n., m.*)	excess
vitesse (*n., f.*)	speed

Everyday English

"The owner's selling it because he lost his driver's license for speeding."

José

—C'est gagné! Jules nous jette les diamants dans leur emballage.

Key Words

gagné (*v.*, gagner *inf.*)	won
jette (*v.*, jeter *inf.*)	throw
diamants (*n.*, *m.*)	diamonds
emballage (*n.*, *m.*)	packaging

Everyday English

"We made it! Jules is throwing us the diamonds in their package!"

Pierre

—Le musée Picasso? . . . C'est par là! . . .

Key Words

musée (*n., m.*)	museum
par là	that way

Everyday English

"The Picasso museum?. . . That way!"

Piédoue

ici, BiENTÔT, CONSTRUCTION D'un PHARE

Key Words

phare (n., m.)   lighthouse

Everyday English

Here, soon, a lighthouse will be built.

Pierre

—Vous n'allez tout de même pas engager comme conseiller un type qui n'a rien entre les oreilles!

Key Words

tout de même	just the same, anyway
conseiller (*n., m.*)	adviser
type (*n., m.*)	guy
oreilles (*n., f.*)	ears
rien (*n., m.*)	nothing

Everyday English

"Anyway, you're not going to hire some guy with nothing between his ears as an adviser!"

Gondot

—Soyons sérieux, Paul, tu n'es pas en état de conduire . . .

Key Words

état (*n., m.*)   state

conduire (*v., inf.*)   drive

Everyday English

"Be serious, Paul, you're in no condition to drive."

Alexandre

—Pour freiner, tu lui appuies sur la tête!

Key Words

freiner (*v., inf.*)	brake
appuies (*v.,* appuyer *inf.*)	push, lean on
tête (*n.,f.*)	head

Everyday English

"To brake, you push on his head!"

Lavergne

—P.S.: excusez mon écriture.

Key Words

écriture (*n., f.*) handwriting

Everyday English

"P.S. Excuse the handwriting."

Harvec

—Maintenant on fait des peintures qui sèchent très rapidement!

Key Words

maintenant	now
fait (*v.*, faire *inf.*)	make
peintures (*n.*, *f.*)	paints
sèchent (*v.*, sécher *inf.*)	dry
rapidement (*adv.*)	quickly

Everyday English

"Nowadays they make paints that dry very fast."

Pierre

—Rien à dire pour les missiles, c'est plutôt au niveau des vecteurs que ça laisse a désirer.

Key Words

rien (*n.*, *m.*)	nothing
dire (*v.*, *inf.*)	say
plutôt (*adv.*)	rather
niveau (*n.*, *m.*)	level
vecteurs (*n.*, *m.*)	delivery systems
laisse (*v.*, laisser *inf.*)	leave

Everyday English

"No complaint about the missiles, it's the delivery system that leaves something to be desired."

Pierre

—On vient pour installer le chauffage central! . . .

Key Words

vient (*v.*, venir *inf.*)	come
chauffage central (*n.*, *m.*)	central heating

Everyday English

"We've come to install the central heating!"

Lavergne

—Pstt! Madame, vous n'auriez pas une épingle de sûreté?
L'élastique de ma culotte est cassé . . .

Key Words

épingle de sûreté (*n., f.*)	safety pin
culotte (*n., f.*)	pants
cassé (*v., casser inf.*)	broken

Everyday English

"Psst! Ma'am, you wouldn't have a safety pin, would you? The
elastic on my pants broke."

Lavergne

—Mais si ça l'amuse, laisse-le jouer avec tes dents. De toute façon, tu n'en as pas besoin maintenant, le repas n'est pas encore prêt!

Key Words

laisse (*v.*, laisser *inf.*)	let
jouer (*v.*, *inf.*)	play
dents (*n.*, *f.*)	teeth
de toute façon	anyway
besoin (*n.*, *m.*)	need
repas (*n.*, *m.*)	meal
prêt (*adj.*)	ready

Everyday English

"So let him play with your teeth if it amuses him. Besides, you don't need them now, the meal's not ready."

Lavergne

—Quand te decideras-tu à acheter un cure-pipe?

Key Words

acheter (*v., inf.*) buy
cure-pipe (*n., m.*) pipe cleaner

Everyday English

"When will you make up your mind to buy a pipe cleaner?"

José

—Chéri, je t'en prie, change de chaîne ou baisse le son . . .

Key Words

chéri (*n., m.*)	dear
prie (*v.*, prier *inf.*)	request
chaîne (*n., m.*)	television channel
baisse (*v.*, baisser *inf.*)	lower
son (*n., m.*)	sound

Everyday English

"Dear, please change the channel or lower the sound."

Pierre

—C'est malin d'envoyer un chapeau sur mon rétroviseur!

Key Words

malin (*adj.*)	smart, clever (sarcastic)
envoyer (*v., inf.*)	send
chapeau (*n., m.*)	hat
rétroviseur (*n., m.*)	rearview mirror

Everyday English

"That's clever—throwing your hat over my rearview mirror!"

Lavergne

—Pour gagner du temps, chère Madame, je crois qu'il serait préférable que vous me donniez votre diagnostic d'abord.

Key Words

gagner (*v., inf.*)	gain
temps (*n., m.*)	time
crois (*v., croire inf.*)	believe
donniez (*v., donner inf.*)	give
diagnostic (*n., m.*)	diagnosis
d'abord (*adv.*)	first

Everyday English

"To save time, my dear lady, I think it would be best if you give me your diagnosis first."

Harvec

Key Words

à part	aside from
bruit (*n., m.*)	noise
mer (*n., f.*)	sea
grand (*adj.*)	great

Everyday English

"I said, aside from the noise of the sea, this place is very quiet."

Piédoue

—Attends un peu de voir la tête du commissaire quand il verra qu'on lui ramène "Pierrot-l'Anguille," le roi de l'évasion.

Key Words

attends (*v.*, attendre *inf.*)	wait
voir (*v.*, *inf.*)	see
tête (*n.*, *f.*)	(in this sense) face
verra (*v.*, voir *inf.*)	will see
ramène (*v.*, ramener *inf.*)	bring back
roi (*n.*, *m.*)	king
évasion (*n.*, *f.*)	escape
anguille (*n.*, *f.*)	eel

Everyday English

"Just wait till we see the face of the Commissioner when we bring in 'Pierrot the Eel,' the escape king."

Lavergne

—Mais oui, tu peux jouer à la pêche, mais, surtout ne réveille pas ton père!

Key Words

peux (*v.*, pouvoir *inf.*)	can
jouer (*v.*, *inf.*)	play
pêche (*n.*, *f.*)	fishing
réveille (*v.*, réveiller *inf.*)	wake
père (*n.*, *m.*)	father

Everyday English

"Yes, you can play fishing, but be sure not to wake your father."

Pierre

—C'est le boss qui sort avec ses gardes du corps!

Key Words

sort (*v.*, sortir *inf.*)   go out

gardes du corps (*n.*, *m.*)   bodyguards

Everyday English

"That's the boss with his bodyguards."

Piédoue

—Et, grâce aux encouragements de son entraîneur, notre concurrent réussit un saut magnifique . . .

Key Words

grâce aux	thanks to
entraîneur (*n., m.*)	trainer
concurrent (*n., m.*)	contestant, competitor
réussit (*v.,* réussir *inf.*)	succeeded
saut (*n., m.*)	jump

Everyday English

"And, with the encouragement of his trainer, our competitor has just succeeded in making a magnificent jump!"

José

—Ne lui donnez pas trop de feuilleté aux amandes, ça le rendrait gourmand!

Key Words

donnez (*v.*, donner *inf.*)	give
feuilleté aux amandes (*n., m.*)	almond puff pastry
rendrait (*v.*, rendre *inf.*)	would make
gourmand (*adj.*)	greedy

Everyday English

"Don't give him too many almond pastries, he pigs out on them!"

Gondot

—Mais je vous ennuie peut-être de vous parler d'économie européenne?

Key Words

ennuie (*v.*, ennuyer *inf.*)   bore
parler (*v.*, *inf.*)   talk about

Everyday English

"But maybe I'm boring you, talking about the European economy..."

José

—Dieu, que j'ai eu peur! J'ai cru qu'il y avait une souris dans le salon . . .

Key Words

Dieu	(Literally: God) Goodness
avoir peur (*v., inf.*)	be afraid
cru (*v.,* croire *inf.*)	thought
souris (*n., f.*)	mouse
salon (*n., m.*)	living room

Everyday English

"Goodness was I scared! I thought there was a mouse in the living room . . ."

Alexandre

—Attention les filles, virage à gauche.

Key Words

attention	careful, watch out
filles (*n., f.*)	girls
virage (*n., m.*)	curve
à gauche	to the left

Everyday English

"Watch out, girls, curve to the left!"

Alexandre

—Devine qui tombe à l'improviste! . . .

Key Words

devine (*v.*, deviner *inf.*)	guess
tombe (*v.*, tomber *inf.*)	fall
à l'improviste	unexpectedly

Everyday English

"Guess who dropped in unexpectedly!"

Lavergne

—Une lettre recommandée, Madame!

Key Words

lettre recommandée (*n., f.*)   registered letter

Everyday English

"Registered letter, m'am!"

Harvec

—Aucune amélioration dans votre amnésie? Vos créanciers commencent à s'impatienter...

Key Words

aucune	not any
amélioration (*n., f.*)	improvement
amnésie (*n., f.*)	amnesia
créanciers (*n., m.*)	creditors
s'impatienter (*v., inf.*)	be impatient

Everyday English

"No improvement of your amnesia? Your creditors are getting impatient."

Gondot

—Prenez bien soin d'enjamber le tapis à chaque fois . . . Il est là pour masquer un trou dans le plancher.

Key Words

enjamber (*v., inf.*)	step over
tapis (*n., m.*)	rug
fois (*n., f.*)	time
masquer (*v., inf.*)	hide
trou (*n., m.*)	hole
plancher (*n., m.*)	floor

Everyday English

"Be careful to step over the rug each time. It's there to hide a hole in the floor."

Pierre

—Les clients du 26 s'en vont? Parfait, leur note est prête!

Key Words

note (*n., f.*)   bill
prête (*adj., f.*)   ready

Everyday English
"The guests in Room 26 are leaving? Fine, their bill is ready!"

Piédoue

—Charles, c'est ton tour de conduire . . .

Key Words

sable (*n., m.*)	sand
tour (*n., m.*)	turn
conduire (*v., inf.*)	drive

Everyday English

Driver of sand truck: "Charles, it's your turn to drive . . ."

Lavergne

—C'est de ma faute, chéri. J'ai oublié de te dire que j'avais savonné les côtés de ce tiroir. Il fallait tellement tirer dessus pour l'ouvrir.

Key Words

faute (*n., f.*)	fault
chéri (*n., m.*)	dear
oublié (*v.,* oublier *inf.*)	forgot
dire (*v., inf.*)	say
savonné (*v.,* savonner *inf.*)	soaped
côtés (*n., m.*)	sides
tiroir (*n., m.*)	drawer
fallait (*v.,* falloir *inf.*)	was necessary
tellement (*adv.*)	so much
tirer (*v., inf.*)	pull
ouvrir (*v., inf.*)	open

Everyday English

"It's my fault, dear! I forgot to tell you that I soaped the sides of that drawer because it was so hard to open."

Piédoue

—Et maintenant, Makengro se précipite pour serrer la main de son heureux vainqueur.

Key Words

se précipite (*v.*, se précipiter *inf.*)	rush, dash
serrer (*v.*, *inf.*)	shake
main (*n.*, *f.*)	hand
heureux (*adj.*)	happy
vainqueur (*n.*, *m.*)	winner

Everyday English

"And now Makengro is jumping the net to shake hands with the happy winner!"

Lavergne

—Vous et vos farces idiotes!

Key Words

farces (*n., f.*)   jokes

Everyday English

"You and your stupid jokes!"

Piédoue

—Plus vite, mon vieux, n'oubliez pas que vous êtes une urgence!

Key Words

vite (*adv.*)	quickly
mon vieux	buddy, pal (in this case, sarcastic)
oubliez (*v.*, oublier *inf.*)	forget

Everyday English

"Faster, pal, don't forget this is an emergency!"

Gondot

—Nom de jeune fille de votre mère?

Key Words

nom de jeune fille (*n., m.*) maiden name
mère (*n., f.*) mother

Everyday English

"Mother's maiden name?"

Pierre

Key Words

haut (*adj.*)	high
mains (*n., f.*)	hands
cernés (*v.*, cerner *inf.*)	surrounded

Everyday English

"Hands up! You're surrounded!"

Pierre

—La région est si déshéritée que les paysans n'arrivent à faire pousser des légumes qu'à la sueur de leur front!

Key Words

déshéritée (*adj.*)	(in this case) poor, low in resources
paysans (*n., m.*)	peasants
arrivent (*v.,* arriver *inf.*)	achieve
faire pousser (*v., inf.*)	grow
légumes (*n., m.*)	vegetables
sueur (*n., f.*)	sweat
front (*n., m.*)	brow

Everyday English

"This region is so poor that the peasants can only grow vegetables by the sweat of their brow!"

Pierre

—On a ordre de surveiller particulièrement Freddy, l'homme caoutchouc!

Key Words

ordre (*n., m.*)	order
surveiller (*v., inf.*)	keep watch over
particulièrement (*adv.*)	particularly
homme (*n., m.*)	man
caoutchouc (*n., m.*)	rubber

Everyday English

"There's an order to keep a close watch on Freddy, the 'rubber man.'"

Alexandre

—Ne souffle plus sur la braise!

Key Words

souffle (*v.*, souffler *inf.*)	blow
braise (*n.*, *f.*)	embers

Everyday English

"Stop blowing on the charcoal!"

Lavergne

—Toujours ses dents! Tu vas voir qu'il va encore nous faire passer une nuit blanche.

Key Words

dents (*n.*, *f.*)	teeth
voir (*v.*, *inf.*)	see
nuit blanche (*n.*, *m.*)	sleepless night
faire (*v.*, *inf.*)	make

Everyday English

"His teeth again! Wait and see—we're going to be up all night again!"

Gondot

—Mais enfin, demandez à votre mari! Je suis sur qu'il est de mon avis . . .

Key Words

demandez (*v.*, demander *inf.*)   ask

mari (*n.*, *m.*)   husband

sûr (*adj.*)   sure

avis (*n.*, *m.*)   opinion

Everyday English

"Go on, ask your husband—I'll bet he agrees with me!"

Key Words

à la maison — at home
bâtir (v., inf.) — construct, build
châteaux (n., m.) — castles

Everyday English

"At home I'll still be able to build sand castles!"

Lavergne

—Toujours pas acheté de séchoir électrique, Monsieur MacIntoch?

Key Words

acheté (*v.*, acheter *inf.*)	bought
séchoir (*n., m.*)	dryer

Everyday English

"Still haven't bought an electric dryer, Mr. MacIntosh?"

Piédoue

"LES SPECTATEURS EN RETARD SONT PRIÉS DE REGAGNER LEUR PLACE SANS DÉRANGER LA PARTIE"

Key Words

en retard (*adj.*)	late
priés (*v.*, prier *inf.*)	requested
regagner (*v.*, *inf.*)	return to
déranger (*v.*, *inf.*)	disturb
partie (*n.*, *f.*)	game

Everyday English

"Latecomers are requested to take their seats without disturbing the game."

Gondot

—De tous mes amis qui ont un chien, je suis le seul à aller chercher mes pantoufles moi-même.

Key Words

amis (*n., m.*)	friends
chien (*n., m.*)	dog
seul (*n., m.*)	only one
chercher (*v., inf.*)	get
pantoufles (*n., f.*)	slippers
moi-même	myself

Everyday English

"Of all my friends who own dogs, I'm the only one who has to go for his own slippers."

Gondot

—C'est gagné . . . Nous ne ferons que dix ans de prison!

Key Words

gagné (*v.*, gagner *inf.*)	won
ferons (*v.*, faire *inf.*)	will do
dix	ten
ans (*n.*, *m.*)	years

Everyday English

"We won—we only got ten years in prison!"

José

—Tu as encore oublié de fermer le gaz . . .

Key Words

oublié (*v.*, oublier *inf.*)	forgot
fermer (*v., inf.*)	shut off
gaz (*n., m.*)	gas

Everyday English

"You forgot to shut off the gas again . . ."

Alexandre

—Il va falloir le réveiller! . . .

Key Words

falloir (*v.*, *inf.*)   be necessary

réveiller (*v.*, *inf.*)   wake up

Everyday English

"I'll have to wake him up!"

José

—Fais attention, la voisine a trouvé une fourmi dans son placard.

Key Words

fais attention (*v.*, faire attention *inf.*)	be careful
voisine (*n., f.*)	neighbor
trouvé (*v.*, trouver *inf.*)	found
fourmi (*n., f.*)	ant
placard (*n., m.*)	closet

Everyday English

"Be careful, the lady next door found an ant in her closet."

Pierre

—Vos craintes n'étaient pas fondées: ce n'est pas un requin mangeur d'hommes!

Key Words

craintes (*n., f.*)	fears
fondées (*adj.*)	founded
requin (*n., m.*)	shark
mangeur d'hommes (*adj.*)	man-eating

Everyday English

"Your fears were unfounded—that's not a man-eating shark!"

Harvec

Key Words

venez (*v.*, venir *inf.*)	come
dire (*v.*, *inf.*)	tell
suivi (*v.*, suivre *inf.*)	follow
régime amaigrissant (*n.*, *m.*)	diet

Everyday English

"Don't come and tell me you've stayed on your diet!"

Key Words

trouve (*v.*, trouver *inf.*)	find
difficilement (*adv.*)	with difficulty
cocktails (*n.*, *m.*)	cocktail parties

Everyday English

"It's hard to find people to serve at cocktail parties."

Alexandre

—Et chez vous, pas trop de dégâts?

Key Words

chez (vous)	at (your place)
dégâts (*n., m.*)	damage

Everyday English

"And you, not too much damage?"

Pierre

—Quel joli temps!

Key Words

joli (*adj.*)   beautiful

temps (*n., m.*)   weather

Everyday English

"What beautiful weather!"

Gondot

—Et si vous avez besoin de quelque chose, n'hésitez pas à aller tirer la cloche dans la cour.

Key Words

besoin (*n., m.*)	need
quelque chose (*n., f.*)	something
tirer (*v., inf.*)	pull
cloche (*n., f.*)	bell
cour (*n., f.*)	courtyard

Everyday English

"And if you need anything, don't hesitate to ring the bell in the courtyard."

Piédoue

—Plantez ça dans le trou pendant que vous y êtes!

Key Words

glace (*n., f.*)	ice
trou (*n., m.*)	hole
pendant que	while

Everyday English

(Sign says: Thin ice.)
"While you're there, put this in the hole."

Pierre

—Et depuis des siècles, les amoureux viennent jeter des pièces d'argent dans ce puits, en gage de leur amour!

Key Words

depuis (*adv.*)	since
siècles (*n., m.*)	centuries
amoureux (*n., m.*)	lovers
jeter (*v., inf.*)	throw
pièces d'argent (*n., f.*)	silver coins
puits (*n., m.*)	well
gage (*n., m.*)	pledge
amour (*n., m.*)	love

Everyday English

"And for centuries now, lovers have been throwing silver coins into this well to pledge their love!"

Harvec

—Ils sont fous! Les inscriptions ont lieu au cinquième étage sans ascenseur . . .

Key Words

fous (*adj., m.*)	crazy
inscriptions (*n., f.*)	registration
ont lieu (*v.,* avoir lieu *inf.*)	take place
cinquième (*adj.*)	fifth
étage (*n., m.*)	floor
ascenseur (*n., m.*)	elevator

Everyday English

"They're crazy! Registration's on the fifth floor and there's no elevator."

Gondot

—Vous permettez que je téléphone à mon avocat?

Key Words

avocat (*n., m.*)   lawyer

Everyday English

"May I phone my lawyer?"

José

—Tu n'aurais pas dû exiger un œuf parfaitement frais . . .

Key Words

dû (*v.*, devoir *inf.*)	should
exiger (*v., inf.*)	insist on
œuf (*n., m.*)	egg
parfaitement (*adv.*)	perfectly
frais (*adj.*)	fresh

Everyday English

"You shouldn't have insisted on a really fresh egg."

Piédoue

—Je te parie que c'est encore un attrape-nigaud!

Key Words

leçons (*n., f.*)	lessons
natation (*n., f.*)	swimming
gratuites (*adj.*)	free
vers (*n., m.*)	worms
asticots (*n., m.*)	grubs
parie (*v.*, parier *inf.*)	bet
attrape-nigaud (*n., m.*)	trick

Everyday English

(Sign says: Free swimming lessons for worms and grubs)
"I'll bet that's just another trick!"

Alexandre

—Je te dis qu'il est fâché maintenant.

Key Words

fâché (*adj.*)   angry, mad

maintenant (*adv.*)   now

Everyday English

"I'm telling you, he's mad now!"

Gondot

—Paul, tu avais du sel ici!

Key Words

sel (*n., m.*)   salt

Everyday English

"Paul, there's salt here!"

Pierre

—Désolé, matricule 20375, mais votre permission du 24 décembre est annulée!

Key Words

désolé	sorry
matricule (*n., m.*)	serial number
permission (*n., f.*)	leave, furlough

Everyday English

"Sorry, Prisoner 20375, but your leave for December 24 is cancelled!"

Gondot

—C'est à votre mari que j'ai demandé d'ouvrir la bouche,
madame . . .

Key Words

mari (*n., m.*)	husband
demande (*v.,* demander *inf.*)	asked
ouvrir (*v., inf.*)	open
bouche (*n., f.*)	mouth

Everyday English

"I asked your *husband* to open his mouth, Madam."

Alexandre

—La fumée ne vous dérange pas?

Key Words

fumée (*n.*, *f.*)   smoke, smoking
dérange (*v.*, déranger *inf.*)   disturb

Everyday English

"My smoking won't disturb you?"

Harvec

—Maintenant que nous avons une décapotable, perds l'habitude de mettre les bagages sur le toit!

Key Words

maintenant	now
décapotable (*n., f.*)	convertible
perds (*v.,* perdre *inf.*)	lose
habitude (*n., f.*)	habit
mettre (*v., inf.*)	put
toit (*n., m.*)	roof

Everyday English

"Now that we've got a convertible, you'll have to get over the habit of putting suitcases on the roof!

Lavergne

—. . . Et, mon Dieu, faites que je sois propre sans être obligé de me laver!

Key Words

Mon Dieu	Dear Lord
faites (*v., faire inf.*)	do, fix
propre (*adj.*)	clean
laver (*v., inf.*)	wash

Everyday English

"And, Dear Lord, fix it so that I can be clean without having to wash!"

Alexandre

—Quelqu'un aurait-il un morceau de fil de fer?

Key Words

morceau (*n., m.*)	piece
fil de fer (*n., m.*)	wire

Everyday English

"Anybody have a piece of wire?"

Piédoue

—Tu peux remonter le poste, la panne d'électricité est réparée.

Key Words

peux (*v.,* pouvoir *inf.*)	can
remonter (*v., inf.*)	put back together
poste (*n., m.*)	television set
panne (*n., f.*)	breakdown
réparée (*v.,* réparer *inf.*)	repaired

Everyday English

"You can put the set back together—the power is on again."

Harvec

—Allez, vas-y, entre! Elle ne va pas te manger.

Key Words

entre (*v.*, entrer *inf.*)	enter
manger (*v.*, *inf.*)	eat

Everyday English

"Go on in, she's not going to eat you!"

Gondot

—Lequel de vous trois a fini la viande froide qui était sur la table?

Key Words

lequel	which one
trois	three
viande (*n., f.*)	meat
froide (*adj.*)	cold

Everyday English

"Which of the three of you finished the cold meat I left on the table?"

Harvec

—On peut choisir?

Key Words

peut (*v.,* pouvoir *inf.*)   can
choisir (*v., inf.*)   choose

Everyday English

"We can choose?"

José

—Mais non, mon mari ne se baigne pas. Il essaie de sortir de la voiture.

Key Words

mari (*n., m.*)	husband
se baigne (*v.*, se baigner *inf.*)	swim
essaie (*v.*, essayer *inf.*)	try
sortir (*v., inf.*)	get out from
voiture	automobile

Everyday English

"No, no, my husband's not swimming. He's trying to get out of the car."

Gondot

—Tu finiras de dormir au bureau ... Il faut que je fasse la chambre.

Key Words

finiras (*v.*, finir *inf.*)	finish
dormir (*v.*, *inf.*)	sleep
bureau (*n.*, *m.*)	office
faut (*v.*, falloir *inf.*)	is necessary
fasse (*v.*, faire *inf.*)	make
chambre (*n.*, *f.*)	bedroom

Everyday English

"You can finish sleeping at the office—I have to straighten up the bedroom."

José

—J'ai cru que j'avais la priorité. Tout le monde peut se tromper.

Key Words

cru (*v.*, croire *inf.*)	thought
priorité (*n.*, *f.*)	right-of-way
peut (*v.*, pouvoir *inf.*)	be able to
se tromper (*v.*, *inf.*)	make a mistake

Everyday English

"I thought I had the right-of-way. Anybody can make a mistake!"

Lavergne

—Vous auriez pu me prévenir que je plongeais à un endroit où on a pied!

—Oui, mais vous savez, dans ce trou, on n'a pas souvent l'occasion de rigoler.

Key Words

pu (*v.*, pouvoir *inf.*)	could
prévenir (*v.*, *inf.*)	warn
plongeais (*v.*, plonger *inf.*)	dived
endroit (*n.*, *m.*)	place
pied (avoir pied)	water shallow enough to stand in
savez (*v.*, savoir *inf.*)	know
trou (*n.*, *m.*)	hole (that is, an unimportant place)
rigoler (*v.*, *inf.*)	laugh at

Everyday English

"You could have warned me before I dived that the water was shallow!"

"Yes, but you know, in these parts we seldom have much to laugh at!"

Piédoue

—Vous n'auriez pas un peu de sucre? On manque de carburant.

Key Words

épicerie (*n., f.*)	grocery store
sucre (*n., m.*)	sugar
manque (*v.,* manquer *inf.*)	lack
carburant (*n., m.*)	fuel

Everyday English

(Sign says: Grocery store)
"Would you have some sugar? We're out of fuel."

Harvec

—Pour te prendre debout, je vais tirer au 500ème!

Key Words

prendre (*v., inf.*)	get
debout (*adv.*)	standing up
tirer (*v., inf.*)	shoot (a picture)

Everyday English

"To get you standing up, I'm going to shoot at five hundred."

Harvec

—Le moteur commence à manquer de puissance.

Key Words

manquer (*v., inf.*)	lack
puissance (*n., f.*)	power

Everyday English

"The motor's beginning to lose power."

Alexandre

—Chéri! . . . assez de canards! . . .

Key Words

chéri	dear
assez (*adv.*)	enough
canards (*n., m.*)	ducks

Everyday English

"Dear—enough ducks!"

Gondot

—On s'était promis de se revoir après les vacances! On a tenu parole . . .

Key Words

promis (*v.*, promettre *inf.*)	promised
se revoir (*v.*, *inf.*)	see one another again
vacances (*n.*, *f.*)	vacation
tenu (*v.*, tenir *inf.*)	kept
parole (*n.*, *f.*)	word

Everyday English

"We promised to see each other after our vacation—we kept our word!"

Piédoue

—Il y a quelqu'un?

Key Words

il y a   there is

quelqu'un   somebody

Everyday English

"Is anybody home?"

French-English Glossary

Verbs are listed in the infinitive form. Reflexive verbs are preceded by *se*. Nouns are listed in singular form unless used in the plural (like *vacances*, vacation).

For additional French words, see "Three Important Verbs," "The Pronouns," and "The Little Words."

In both glossaries, the entries are followed by the pages on which the words can be found.

acheter to buy, 30, 61

agence agency, 16

amélioration improvement, 45

ami friend, 63

amnésie amnesia, 45

amour love, 75

amoureux lover, 75

an year, 64

anguille eel, 35

à part aside from, 34

apprendre to learn, 10

appuyer to push, to lean on, 23

arriver à to achieve, 55

ascenseur elevator, 76

assez enough, 99

asticot grub, 79

attendre to wait for, 35

attention careful, watch out, 42; **faire attention** to be careful, 67

attrape-nigaud trick, 79

aucun not any, 45

avis opinion, 59

avocat lawyer, 77

avoir lieu to take place, 76

se baigner to swim, 92

baisser to lower, 31

bâtir to build, 60

bavarder to chat, gossip, 11

besoin need, 29, 73

boîte box, 15

boîte à gants glove compartment, 15

bouche mouth, 83

braise embers, 57

bruit noise, 34

bureau office, 93

café coffee, 13

canard duck, 99

caoutchouc rubber, 56

carburant fuel, 96

casser to break, 28

cerner to surround, 54

chaîne television channel, 31

chambre bedroom, 93

chapeau hat, 32

château castle, 60

chauffage central central heating, 27

chercher to get, 63

chéri dear, 31, 49, 99

chez (vous) at (your place), 71

chien dog, 63

choisir to choose, 91

chose thing, 73

cinquième fifth, 76

cloche bell, 73

cocktail cocktail party, 70

compteur à gaz gas meter, 14

concurrent contestant, competitor, 38

conduire to drive, 17, 22, 48

conseiller adviser, 21

côté side, 49

cour courtyard, 73

craindre to be afraid of, 7

crainte fear, 68

créancier creditor, 45

croire to believe; to think, 33, 41, 94

cuir leather, 6

culotte pants, 28

cure-pipe pipe cleaner, 30

d'abord first, 33

débloquer to release, 15

debout standing up, 97

décapotable convertible, 85

dégât damage, 71

demander to ask, 59, 83

dent tooth, 29, 58

départ departure, 12

depuis since, 75

déranger to disturb, 62, 84

désherité poor, 55

désolé sorry, 82

désormais from now on, 13

de toute façon anyway, 29

devenir to become, 4

deviner to guess, 43

devoir to have to, should, 78

diagnostic diagnosis, 33

diamant diamond, 18

Dieu Goodness (God), 41

difficilement with difficulty, 70

dire to tell, to say, 1, 26, 49, 69

dix ten, 64

donc therefore, 9

donner to give, 33, 39

dormir to sleep, 93

école school, 1

écriture handwriting, 24

emballage packaging, 18

endroit place, 95

enjamber to step over, 46

ennuyer to bore, 40

en retard late, 62

entraîneur trainer, 38

entrer to enter, 89

envoyer to send, 32

épicerie grocery store, 96

épingle de sûreté safety pin, 28

essayer to try, 92

étage floor, 76

état state, 22

évasion escape, 35

excès excess, 17

exiger to insist on, 78

fâché angry, 80

façon, de toute anyway, 29

facteur postman, 7

faillir to come near, 12

faire to do, 5, 64, 86; to make, 9, 25, 58, 93

faire attention to be careful, 67

faire pousser to grow (vegetables), 55

falloir to be necessary, 49, 66, 93

farce joke, 51

faute fault, 49

fermer to shut off, 65

feuilleté aux amandes almond puff pastry, 39

fil de fer wire, 87

fille girl, 42

finir to finish, 93

fois time, 46

fondé founded, 68

fou crazy, 76

fourmi ant, 67

frais fresh, 78

frein brake, 15

freiner to brake, 23

froid cold, 90

front brow, 55

fuite leak, 3

fumée smoke, smoking, 84

gage pledge, 75

gagner to win, 18, 64; to gain, 33

gant glove, 15

garde du corps bodyguard, 37

gauche, à to the left, 42

gaz gas, 65

glace ice, 74

gourmand greedy, 39

grâce à thanks to, 38

grand great, 34

gratuit free, 79

gros big, 15

habitude habit, 85

haut high, 54

heureux happy, 50

homme man, 56

huit eight, 8

il y a there is, 101

s'impatienter to be impatient, 45

improviste, à l' unexpectedly, 43

inscription registration, 76

instituteur teacher, 1

jeter to throw, 18, 75

joli beautiful, 72

jouer to play, 2, 4, 29, 36

jour day, 7

laisser to let, 4, 29; to leave, 26

laver to wash, 86

leçon lesson, 79

légume vegetable, 55

lequel which one, 90

lettre recommandée registered letter, 44

lourd heavy, 9

main hand, 15, 50, 54

maintenant now, 25, 80, 85

maison, à la at home, 60

malin smart, clever, 32

manger to eat, 89

mangeur d'hommes man-eating, 68

manquer to lack, 96, 98

mari husband, 59, 83, 92

masquer to hide, 46

matricule serial number, 82

mazout oil, 3

mer sea, 12, 34

mère mother, 53

mettre to put, 85

moi-même myself, 63

Mon Dieu Dear Lord, 86

mon vieux buddy, pal, 52

morceau piece, 87

mordre to bite, 7

musée museum, 18

nager to swim, 10

natation swimming, 79

niveau level, 26

noir black, 15

nom de jeune fille maiden name, 53

note bill, 47

nuit blanche sleepless night, 58

œuf egg, 78

ordre order, 56

oreille ear, 21

oublier to forget, 49, 52, 65

ouvrir to open, 49, 83

panne breakdown, 88

pantoufle slipper, 63

paraître to seem, 3

parfaitement perfectly, 78

parier to bet, 79

par là that way, 19

parler to talk, 40

parole word, 5, 100

particulièrement particularly, 56

partie game, 62

paysan peasant, 55

pêche fishing, 7, 36

peinture paint, 25

pendant que while, 74

perdre to lose, 85

père father, 36

permis license, 7

permis de conduire driver's license, 17

permission leave, furlough, 82

peur, avoir to be afraid, 41

phare lighthouse, 20

pièce d'argent silver coin, 75

pied, avoir to be in shallow water, 95

placard closet, 67

plancher floor, 46

plonger to dive, 95

plusieurs several, many, 9

plutôt rather, instead of, 26

poignée handle, 15

poste television set, 88

pouvoir to be able to, can, 36, 88, 91, 94, 95

se précipiter to rush, dash, 50

prendre to get, 97

prêt (n.) loan, 16

prêt, prête (adj.) ready, 29, 47

prévenir to warn, 95

prier to request, 31, 62

priorité right-of-way, 94

promettre to promise, 100

propre clean, 86

propriétaire owner, 17

puissance power, 98

puits well, 75

quelque chose something, 73

quelqu'un somebody, 101

ramener to bring back, 35

rapidement quickly, 25

rater to miss, 12

regagner to return to, 62

régime amaigrissant diet, 69

relever to take a reading, 14

remettre to deliver; to give, 13

remonter to put back together, 88

rendre to repay, 16; to make, to render, 39

réparer to repair, 88

repas meal, 29

requin shark, 68

retirer to withdraw, 17

rétroviseur rearview mirror, 32

réussir to succeed, 38

réveiller to wake (someone) up, 36, 66

se revoir to see each other again, 100

rien nothing, 21, 26

rigoler to laugh at, 95

roi king, 35

sable sand, 48

salle des machines engine room, 3

salon living room, 41

saut jump, 38

savoir to know, 95

savonner to soap, 49

sécher to dry, 25

séchoir dryer, 61

sel salt, 81

serrer (la main) to shake (hands), 50

seul single, only one, 13, 63

siècle century, 75

son sound, 31

sortir to go out, 37; to get out from, 92

souffler to blow, 57

souris mouse, 41

sucre sugar, 13, 96

sueur sweat, 55

suivre to follow, 69

sûr sure, 59

surveiller to watch over, 56

tapis rug, 46

tellement so much, 49

temps time, 33; weather, 72

tenir to keep, 100

tête head, 23; face, 35

tirer to pull, 49, 73; to shoot (a picture), 97

tiroir drawer, 49

toi-même yourself, 1

toit roof, 85

tomber to fall, 43

tour turn, 14, 48

tout d'abord first of all, 10

tout de même just the same; anyway, 21

traverser to undergo, 13

trois three, 90

se tromper to make a mistake, 94

trou hole, 48, 74, 95

trouver to find, 67, 70; **se trouver** to be located, 14

type guy, 21

vacances vacation, 100

vainqueur winner, 50

vecteur delivery system, 26

vendre to sell, 17

venir to come, 1, 14, 27, 69

ver worm, 79

viande meat, 90

virage curve, 42

vite quickly, 4, 52

vitesse speed, 17

voir to see, 4, 11, 35, 58

voisine neighbor, 67

voiture car, 92

vouloir to want, 5

voyage trip, 9

yeux eyes, 6

English-French Glossary

able, be   pouvoir, 36, 91, 95

achieve   arriver à, 55

adviser   le conseiller, 21

afraid, be   craindre, 7; avoir peur, 41

agency   l'agence, 16

amnesia   l'amnésie, 45

angry   fâché, 80

ant   la fourmi, 67

anyway   tout de même, 21; de toute façon, 29

aside from   à part, 34

ask   demander, 59, 83

at (place)   chez, 71

automobile   la voiture, 92

be able   pouvoir, 94

beautiful   joli, 72

become   devenir, 4

bedroom   la chambre, 93

believe   croire, 33

bell   la cloche, 73

bet   parier, 79

big   gros, 15

bill   la note, 47

bite   mordre, 7

black   noir, 15

blow   souffler, 57

bodyguard   le garde du corps, 37

bore   ennuyer, 40

box   la boîte, 15

brake (n.)   le frein, 15

brake (v.)   freiner, 23

break   casser, 28

breakdown   la panne, 88

bring back   ramener, 35

brow   le front, 55

buddy   mon vieux, 52

build   bâtir, 60

buy   acheter, 30, 61

can (v.)   pouvoir, 36, 88, 91, 95

careful   attention, 42; **be careful**   faire attention, 67

castle   le château, 60

central heating   le chauffage central, 27

century   le siècle, 75

channel, television   la chaîne, 31

choose   choisir, 91

clean (adj.)   propre, 86

clever   malin, 32

closet   le placard, 67

cocktail party   le cocktail, 70

coffee   le café, 13

cold   froid, 90

come   venir, 1, 14, 27, 69

come near   faillir, 12

competitor   le concurrent, 38

construct   bâtir, 60

contestant   le concurrent, 38

convertible   la décapotable, 85

courtyard   la cour, 73

crazy   fou, 76

creditor   le créancier, 45

curve   le virage, 42

damage   le dégât, 71

dash   se précipiter, 50

day   jour, 8

dear chéri, 31, 49, 99

Dear Lord Mon Dieu, 86

deliver remettre, 13

delivery system le vecteur, 26

departure le départ, 12

diagnosis le diagnostic, 33

diamond le diamant, 18

diet le régime amaigrissant, 69

difficulty, with difficilement, 70

disturb déranger, 62, 84

dive plonger, 95

do faire, 5, 64, 86

dog le chien, 63

drawer le tiroir, 49

drive conduire, 22, 48

driver's license le permis de conduire, 17

dry sécher, 25

dryer le séchoir, 61

duck le canard, 99

ear l'oreille, 21

eat manger, 89

eel l'anguille, 35

egg l'œuf, 78

eight huit, 8

elevator l'ascenseur, 76

embers la braise, 57

engine room la salle des machines, 3

enough assez, 99

enter entrer, 89

escape l'évasion, 35

excess l'excès, 17

eyes les yeux, 6

face la tête, 35

fall tomber, 43

father le père, 36

fault la faute, 49

fear la crainte, 68

fifth cinquième, 76

find trouver, 67, 70

finish finir, 93

first tout d'abord, 10; d'abord, 33

fishing la pêche, 8, 36

fix faire, 86

floor le plancher, 46; l'étage, 76

follow suivre, 69

forget oublier, 49, 52, 65

founded fondé, 68

free gratuit, 79

fresh frais, 78

friend l'ami, 63

from now on désormais, 13

fuel le carburant, 96

furlough la permission, 82

gain gagner, 33

game la partie, 62

gas le gaz, 65

gas meter le compteur à gaz, 14

get prendre, 97; chercher, 63

get out from sortir, 92

girl la fille, 42

give donner, 33, 39; remettre, 13

glove le gant, 15

glove compartment la boîte à gants, 15

Goodness Dieu, 41

go out sortir, 37

gossip bavarder, 11

great grand, 34

greedy gourmand, 39

grocery store l'épicerie, 96

grow (vegetables) faire pousser, 55

grub l'asticot, 79

guess deviner, 43

guy le type, 21

habit l'habitude, 85

hand la main, 15, 50, 54

handle la poignée, 15

handwriting l'écriture, 24

happy heureux, 50

hat le chapeau, 32

head la tête, 23

heating, central le chauffage central, 27

heavy lourd, 9

hide masquer, 46

high haut, 54

hole le trou, 46, 74, 95

home, at à la maison, 60

husband le mari, 59, 83, 92

ice la glace, 74

impatient, be s'impatienter, 45

improvement l'amélioration, 45

insist on exiger, 78

joke la farce, 51

jump le saut, 38

just the same tout de même, 21

keep tenir, 100

king le roi, 35

know savoir, 95

lack (v.) manquer, 96, 98

late en retard, 62

laugh at rigoler, 95

lawyer l'avocat, 77

leak la fuite, 3

lean on appuyer, 23

learn apprendre, 10

leather le cuir, 6

leave (v.) laisser, 26

leave (n.) la permission, 82

left, to the à gauche, 42

lesson la leçon, 79

let laisser, 4, 29

letter, registered la lettre recommandée, 44

level le niveau, 26

license le permis, 8

lighthouse le phare, 20

living room le salon, 41

loan le prêt, 16

located, to be se trouver, 14

lose perdre, 85

love l'amour, 75

lover l'amoureux, 75

lower baisser, 31

mad fâché, 80

maiden name le nom de jeune fille, 53

make faire, 9, 25, 58, 93; rendre, 39

man l'homme, 56

man-eating mangeur d'hommes, 68

many plusieurs, 9

meal repas, 29

meat   la viande, 90

mirror, rearview   le rétroviseur, 32

miss (v.)   rater, 12

mistake, make a   se tromper, 94

mother   la mère, 53

mouse   la souris, 41

mouth   la bouche, 83

museum   le musée, 19

myself   moi-même, 63

necessary, be   falloir, 49, 66, 93

need   le besoin, 29, 73

neighbor   la voisine, 67

noise   le bruit, 34

not any   aucun, 45

nothing   rien, 21, 26

now   maintenant, 25, 80, 85

office   le bureau, 93

oil   le mazout, 3

only one   le seul, 13, 63

open   ouvrir, 49, 83

opinion   l'avis, 59

order   l'ordre, 56

owner   le propriétaire, 17

packaging   l'emballage, 18

paint   la peinture, 25

pal   mon vieux, 52

pants   la culotte, 28

particularly   particulièrement, 56

pastry   le feuilleté, 39

peasant   le paysan, 55

perfectly   parfaitement, 78

piece   le morceau, 87

pipe cleaner   le cure-pipe, 30

place   l'endroit, 95

play   jouer, 2, 4, 29, 36

pledge   le gage, 75

poor   désherité, 55

postman   le facteur, 7

power   la puissance, 98

promise   promettre, 100

pull   tirer, 49, 73

push   appuyer, 23

put   mettre, 85

put back together   remonter, 88

quickly   vite, 4, 52; rapidement, 25

rather   plutôt, 26

reading, take a   relever, 14

ready   prêt, prête, 29, 47

rearview mirror   le rétroviseur, 32

registered letter   la lettre recommandée, 44

registration   l'inscription, 76

release   débloquer, 15

repair   réparer, 88

repay   rendre, 16

request   prier, 31, 62

return to   regagner, 62

right-of-way   priorité, 94

roof   le toit, 85

rubber   le caoutchouc, 56

rug   le tapis, 46

rush   se précipiter, 50

safety pin   l'épingle de sûreté, 28

salt   le sel, 81

sand   le sable, 48

say dire, 1, 26, 49

school l'école, 1

sea la mer, 12, 34

see voir, 4, 11, 35, 58

see each other again se revoir, 100

seem paraître, 3

sell vendre, 17

send envoyer, 32

serial number la matricule, 82

shake (hands) serrer (la main), 50

shark le requin, 68

shoot (pictures) tirer, 97

should devoir, 78

shut off fermer, 65

side le côté, 49

silver coin la pièce d'argent, 75

since depuis, 75

single seul, 13

sleep dormir, 93

sleepless night la nuit blanche, 58

slipper la pantoufle, 63

smart malin, 32

smoke, smoking la fumée, 84

soap (v.) savonner, 49

somebody quelqu'un, 101

something quelque chose, 73

so much tellement, 49

sorry désolé, 82

sound le son, 31

speed la vitesse, 17

standing up debout, 97

state l'état, 22

step over enjamber, 46

succeed gagner 13, 64; réussir, 38

sugar le sucre, 13, 96

sure sûr, 59

surround cerner, 54

sweat la sueur, 55

swim nager, 10; se baigner, 92

swimming la natation, 79

take a reading relever, 14

take place avoir lieu, 76

talk parler, 40; bavarder, 11

teacher l'instituteur, 1

television channel la chaîne, 31

television set le poste, 88

tell dire, 69

ten dix, 64

thanks to grâce à, 38

that way par là, 19

therefore donc, 9

there is il y a, 101

thing la chose, 73

think croire, 41, 94

three trois, 90

throw jeter, 18, 75

time le temps 33; la fois, 46

tooth la dent, 29, 58

trainer l'entraîneur, 38

trick l'attrape-nigaud, 79

trip le voyage, 9

try essayer, 92

turn le tour, 14, 48

undergo traverser, 13

unexpectedly à l'improviste, 43

vacation   les vacances, 100

vegetable   le légume, 55

wait   attendre, 35

wake (someone) up
réveiller, 36, 66

want   vouloir, 5

warn   prévenir, 95

wash   laver, 86

watch out   attention, 42

watch over   surveiller, 56

water, shallow   eau où l'on a
pied, 95

weather   le temps, 72

well   le puits, 75

which one   lequel, 90

while   pendant que, 74

win   gagner, 18, 64

winner   le vainqueur, 50

wire   le fil de fer, 87

withdraw   retirer, 17

word   la parole, 5, 100

worm   le ver, 79

year   l'an, 64

yourself   toi-même, 1

English-French Subject Index

People and Characteristics

adviser le conseiller, 21

beautiful joli, 72

big gros, 15

black noir, 15

bodyguard le garde du corps, 37

brow le front, 55

clean propre, 86

competitor le concurrent, 38

contestant le concurrent, 38

crazy fou, 76

creditor le créancier, 45

dear chéri, 31, 49, 99

ear l'oreille, 21

eyes les yeux, 6

face la tête, 35

father le père, 36

friend l'ami, 63

girl la fille, 42

great grand, 34

guy le type, 21

hand la main, 15, 50, 54

head la tête, 23

heavy lourd, 9

husband le mari, 59, 83, 92

king le roi, 35

lawyer l'avocat, 77

lover l'amoureux, 75

maiden name le nom de jeune fille, 53

man l'homme, 56

mother la mère, 53

mouth la bouche, 83

myself moi-même, 63

neighbor la voisine, 67

owner le propriétaire, 17

peasant le paysan, 55

postman le facteur, 7

smart malin, 32

somebody quelqu'un, 101

teacher l'instituteur, 1

tooth la dent, 29, 58

trainer l'entraîneur, 38

winner le vainqueur, 50

yourself toi-même, 1

When and How Much?

century le siècle, 75

day le jour, 8

eight huit, 8

enough assez, 99

excess l'excès, 17

fifth cinquième, 76

finish finir, 93

first d'abord, 10, 33

free gratuit, 79

from now on désormais, 13

lack manquer, 96, 98

late en retard, 62

many plusieurs, 9

miss rater, 12

not any aucun, 45

nothing rien, 21, 26

now   maintenant, 25, 80, 85

only one   le seul, 13, 63

piece   le morceau, 87

quickly   vite, 4, 52;
  rapidement, 25

ready   prêt, 29, 47

serial number   la matricule,
  82

since   depuis, 75

single   seul, 13

sleepless night   la nuit
  blanche, 58

so much   tellement, 49

ten   dix, 64

three   trois, 90

time   le temps, 33; la fois,
  46

wait   attendre, 35

wake (someone) up   réveiller,
  36, 66

which one   lequel, 90

while   pendant que, 74

year   l'an, 64

Where and How to Go

agency   l'agence, 16

at (place)   chez, 71

bedroom   la chambre, 93

castle   le château, 60

closet   le placard, 67

cocktail party   le cocktail, 70

come   venir, 1, 14, 27, 69

come near   faillir, 12

courtyard   la cour, 73

curve   le virage, 42

dash   se précipiter, 50

dive   plonger, 95

drive   conduire, 22, 48

elevator   l'ascenseur, 76

engine room   la salle des
  machines, 3

enter   entrer, 89

escape   l'évasion, 35

fall   tomber, 43

find   trouver, 67, 70

floor   le plancher, 46; l'étage,
  76

follow   suivre, 69

fuel   le carburant, 96

go   chercher, 63

get out from   sortir, 92

go out   sortir, 37

hide   masquer, 46

high   haut, 54

hole   le trou, 46, 74, 95

home, at   à la maison, 60

jump   sauter, 38

leave   laisser, 26

left, to the   à gauche, 42

level   le niveau, 26

lighthouse   le phare, 20

living room   le salon, 41

located, to be   se trouver,
  14

lose   perdre, 85

lower   baisser, 31

museum   le musée, 19

office   le bureau, 93

place   l'endroit, 95

return to   regagner, 62

school l'école, 1

sea la mer, 12, 34

shallow water eau où l'on a pied, 95

side le côté, 49

speed la vitesse, 17

standing up debout, 97

step over enjamber, 46

swim nager, 10; se baigner, 92

swimming la natation, 79

that way par là, 19

trip le voyage, 9

turn le tour, 14, 48

vacation les vacances, 100

withdraw retirer, 17

At Home

ant la fourmi, 67

automobile la voiture, 92

bell la cloche, 73

bill la note, 47

box la boîte, 15

coffee le café, 13

convertible la décapotable, 85

dog le chien, 63

drawer le tiroir, 49

driver's license le permis de conduire, 17

dryer le séchoir, 61

egg l'œuf, 78

embers la braise, 57

game la partie, 62

gas le gaz, 65

gas meter le compteur à gaz, 14

handle la poignée, 15

handwriting l'écriture, 24

hat le chapeau, 32

heating, central le chauffage central, 27

ice la glace, 74

leak la fuite, 3

leather le cuir, 6

letter, registered la lettre recommandée, 44

license le permis, 8

meal le repas, 29

meat la viande, 90

mirror, rearview le rétroviseur, 32

mouse la souris, 41

oil le mazout, 3

packaging l'emballage, 18

paint la peinture, 25

pants la culotte, 28

pipe cleaner le cure-pipe, 30

roof le toit, 85

rubber le caoutchouc, 56

rug le tapis, 46

safety pin l'épingle de sûreté, 28

salt le sel, 81

slipper la pantoufle, 63

sound le son, 31

sugar le sucre, 13, 96

television channel la chaîne, 31

television set le poste, 88

vegetable le légume, 55

well le puits, 75

wire le fil de fer, 87

Thoughts and Feelings

afraid, be   craindre, 7; avoir peur, 41

angry   fâché, 80

believe   croire, 33

choose   choisir, 91

Dear Lord   Mon Dieu, 86

fault   la faute, 49

fear   la crainte, 68

forget   oublier, 49, 52, 65

Goodness   Dieu, 41

guess   deviner, 43

happy   heureux, 50

impatient, be   s'impatienter, 45

joke   la farce, 51

know   savoir, 95

learn   apprendre, 10

love   l'amour, 75

need   le besoin, 29, 73

opinion   l'avis, 59

power   la puissance, 98

seem   paraître, 3

sorry   désolé, 82

sure   sûr, 59

thanks to   grâce à, 38

think   croire, 41, 94

want   vouloir, 5

People among Themselves

anyway   tout de même, 21; de toute façon, 29

aside from   à part, 34

ask   demander, 59, 83

bet   parier, 79

bore   ennuyer, 40

careful, be   faire attention, 67

diagnosis   le diagnostic, 33

disturb   déranger, 62, 84

gossip   bavarder, 11

insist on   exiger, 78

laugh at   rigoler, 95

lesson   la leçon, 79

let   laisser, 4, 29

mistake, make a   se tromper, 94

noise   le bruit, 34

order   l'ordre, 56

pledge   le gage, 75

promise   promettre, 100

registration   l'inscription, 76

repay   rendre, 16

request   prier, 31, 62

say   dire, 1, 26, 49

shake (hands)   serrer (la main), 50

surround   cerner, 54

sweat   la sueur, 55

talk   parler, 40; bavarder, 11

tell   dire, 69

therefore   donc, 9

warn   prévenir, 95

watch over   surveiller, 56

weather   le temps, 72

word   la parole, 5, 100

People and Things

bite mordre, 7

blow souffler, 57

brake le frein, 15; freiner, 23

break casser, 28

breakdown la panne, 88

bring back ramener, 35

damage le dégât, 71

dry sécher, 25

eat manger, 89

founded fondé, 68

man-eating mangeur d'hommes, 68

open ouvrir, 49, 83

pull tirer, 49, 73

push appuyer, 23

put back together remonter, 88

reading, take a relever, 14

release débloquer, 15

repair réparer, 88

sell vendre, 17

send envoyer, 32

shoot tirer, 97

shut off fermer, 65

smoke, smoking la fumée, 84

soap savonner, 49

take place avoir lieu, 76

throw jeter, 18, 75

undergo traverser, 13

wash laver, 86

Positive and Negative Actions

achieve arriver à, 55

amnesia l'amnésie, 45

be able pouvoir, 94

become devenir, 4

build bâtir, 60

buy acheter, 30, 61

cold froid, 90

difficulty, with difficilement, 70

do faire, 5, 64, 86

fishing la pêche, 8, 36

fresh frais, 78

gain gagner, 33

get prendre, 97; chercher, 63

give donner, 33, 39

grow faire pousser, 55

habit l'habitude, 85

improvement l'amélioration, 45

keep tenir, 100

make faire, 9, 25, 58, 93

necessary, be falloir, 49, 66, 93

particularly particulièrement, 56

perfectly parfaitement, 78

play jouer, 2, 4, 29, 36

poor déshérité, 55

rather plutôt, 26

see each other again se revoir, 100

should devoir, 78

sleep dormir, 93

state l'état, 22

succeed   gagner, 13, 64;
  réussir, 38

try   essayer, 92

unexpectedly   à l'improviste,
  43

win   gagner, 18, 64

What Things?

delivery system   le vecteur,
  26

diamond   le diamant, 18

duck   le canard, 99

eel   l'anguille, 35

glove   le gant, 15

grocery store   l'épicerie, 96

grub   l'asticot, 79

loan   le prêt, 16

sand   le sable, 48

shark   le requin, 68

silver coin   la pièce d'argent,
  75

something   quelque chose, 73

thing   la chose, 73

trick   l'attrape-nigaud, 79

well   le puits, 75

worm   le ver, 79